BLOCKCHAIN TECHNOLOGY EXPLAINED

THE ULTIMATE BEGINNER'S GUIDE ABOUT BLOCKCHAIN WALLET, MINING, BITCOIN, ETHEREUM, LITECOIN, ZCASH, MONERO, RIPPLE, DASH, IOTA AND SMART CONTRACTS

ALAN T. NORMAN

Get Your Free **Cryptocurrency Mining** Bonus Book

(Find it in the end of a book)

TABLE OF CONTENTS

WHY YOU SHOULD READ THIS BOOK

If you've never heard of blockchain or you only have a vague idea of how this new technology works, this is the book for you. In this short guide I'll walk you through the essentials of how blockchain technology works, using simple explanations and giving examples along the way. I've introduced many people to blockchain, so I know where beginners usually get confused and the main questions they have. All of the basic principles are addressed step-by-step in this book.You don't need any special knowledge or understanding of technology to understand the concepts in this book. Blockchain is a technology, like the internet or the personal computer, that's intended for use by the masses. It holds the potential to revolutionize almost every interaction in our lives.Many readers will have heard of Bitcoin and cryptocurrencies. These are an important application of blockchain technology and the first application. However, blockchain is not restricted to use in finance and payment systems. While we'll definitely cover Bitcoin and other cryptocurrencies in this book, we'll also look at potential applications of blockchain across many different industries.

THIS IS NOT A BOOK ABOUT INVESTING IN BITCOIN OR OTHER CRYPTOCURRENCIES

Over the past few years, hundreds of new currencies have been created, all living online, on the blockchain. For newcomers to the technology, it may come as a surprise that people are seriously investing in newly-invented digital currencies like Bitcoin.While these currencies are interesting and have potential to gain wide usage, this is not a book about cryptocurrency. If you're looking for investing advice or insider information about which currencies will be most successful, you will not find it in this book, you would read my another book – **Cryptocurrency Investing Bible" (http://amzn.to/2zzB8IP).**

For those of you who are new to blockchain, the idea of investing in cryptocurrency might sound appealing. A word of warning: investing in cryptocurrency is a highly volatile market and extremely risky. Do your research before investing in a cryptocurrency to make sure it is legitimate, and don't invest any more money than you can afford to lose. Blockchain and cryptocurrencies are still in the early days, and anything could happen at any time.

WHAT YOU WILL LEARN IN THIS BOOK

Instead of talking about investing, this book will focus on how blockchain technology works and how it might be used in the future. Topics you can expect to see in this book include:

- ☐ What problem does blockchain solve?

- How can technology make our institutions faster and less expensive?
- Could technology replace our institutions (like governments, banks, etc) altogether?
- How does blockchain build trust between strangers?
- How does blockchain increase security for transactions and contracts?
- Can blockchain be used outside of finance?
- What is a block?
- What is the chain and why do we need it?
- What's a technical explanation of what happens in the blockchain?
- What is mining and why do we need it?
- Are there alternatives to mining to create a blockchain?
- What's the story of Bitcoin?
- Does Bitcoin have any problems?
- What is Ethereum, and what is a smart contract?
- Are there other blockchain technologies I should know about?
- How are companies adopting blockchain?
- What regulatory hurdles might slow blockchain adoption?

Whew, that's a lot of questions. If you're ready to tackle them, I'm ready. Let's get started.

WHAT DOES THE BLOCKCHAIN DO?

Before we get into any of the technical details behind blockchain technology, it's important to understand the problems that blockchain solves. Why do we need blockchain, and what does it do that our current technology can't do?The early adopters of Bitcoin and blockchain technology spotted what they perceived as a fundamental flaw in the way we think about transactions, trust, and social institutions. The earliest versions of blockchain came right around the same time as the 2007 financial crisis in the United States, when many people lost faith in societal institutions that were supposed to protect the interests of the common man. Of course, people were disillusioned by the banking system in the wake of the crisis, but they also lost faith in government to regulate financial markets and in the press to investigate potential crises.In fact, Gallup polls (http://news.gallup.com/poll/1597/confidence-institutions.aspx) and the Edelman Trust Barometer (https://www.edelman.com/trust2017/) both show a steady decline in the public's trust in institutions-- banks, government, media, academia, and nonprofits-- over the past decade. Trust in institutions is at an all-time low in American history, and similar issues plague the E.U. (Brexit, Marine Le Pen's rise, Catalonian independence, Greece's governance crisis).The foundational idea behind institutions is creating trust between strangers in society. We have laws and systems in place to make it possible for millions of people who don't know each other to live in proximity to one another. However, the creators of blockchain felt these institutions were failing.

THE PROBLEM WITH INSTITUTIONS

To see why blockchain's creators want to replace institutions, it's useful to think about how we got to the point where institutional trust is so low. What weaknesses do institutions have, and how might blockchain solve them?

SLOW

The first and biggest institutional weakness is speed. Institutions, by their very nature, are slow. They require approvals and multiple rounds of verification for every relationship, contract, and transaction. Policy changes at an institutional level are also slow. It can take months or years to create new laws or implement new procedures.For example, filing your tax return takes hours of work and headache. Then, the government has to verify the information you've included in the return before you receive your refund. Months or even years later, the government may choose to audit you, in which case you'll need copies of old financial transactions from several years ago.

Another example is banking transaction times. There's no reason, technologically, why a bank transfer should take more than a few minutes. However, it usually takes a few business days for a transaction to clear because of a combination of outdated systems, internal policies, and government regulations that require the transaction be analyzed and processed.Blockchain technology is governed by its users and utilizes cryptography to maintain user privacy. Depending on how the system is designed, it can be incredibly fast. New smart contracts can automatically calculate and disburse something like a tax return or even a business invoice once certain conditions are met. Since it's consensus based, the community can collectively decide to implement a change in the way the system runs, addressing problems as they arise.

EXPENSIVE

Traditional institutions are also expensive. It's easy to point to taxes as one expense of institutions, but all the transaction fees and user subscriptions you pay each month are other forms of institutional expenses. Over time, those expenses add up.For example, banks charge fees to process wire transfers, convert currencies, or even manage your account. Insurance agencies require administrative fees that are built into your insurance premiums. Many online retailers charge credit card transaction fees. If you run a small business, you'll find fees everywhere from marketing to payment processing. We've become so accustomed to these small fees as the cost of living in society, but blockchain hopes to challenge that assumption.Blockchain contracts and transactions take place on a shared network. The users on the network also pitch in to verify the transactions of others. Instead of a central authority charging a fee to verify your transaction, you verify another transaction on the network in exchange for your own transaction getting processed. Not all blockchain technologies work exactly this way, but the idea is the same for most. By participating in the network, you end up with fewer fees than you would have paid a traditional institution.

SUBJECT TO ATTACK

Cybercrime is on the rise, (http://on.inc.com/2EynUzS) and it's now common to hear about major institutions getting hacked or having personal data breaches. Vulnerability to attacks is one of the reasons trust in institutions is declining. When you centralize data, you're sure to find bad actors looking to capitalize on that information.

2017's Equifax hack (http://cnnmon.ie/2Evg6e7) in the United States is one major example. Equifax collects credit information on consumers in the United States, including credit card numbers, social security information, full names, addresses, and payment history. The data breach in September 2017 affected 143 million consumers, highlighting the dangers of trusting data security to a major institution.Blockchain technologies use multiple layers of cryptography to protect user information. Some blockchain technologies are more secure than others, and each technology has its own method for ensuring privacy. However, since each relationship, contract, and transaction is individually encrypted, even if you were to breach one piece of personal information, you wouldn't gain access to anyone else's information in the process.

REPLACING INSTITUTIONS WITH TECHNOLOGY

Most would agree that our institutions have flaws and aren't perfect solutions. But they do solve problems of trust, and they've been doing it for hundreds of years. In fact, we're probably living in the most peaceful, comfortable era (http://slate.me/2HgHzSq) in human history. Any alternative to our current institutions needs to have clear advantages and strength.The idea behind blockchain is to replace institutions with technology that can do the job better and empowers individuals. If you could create a way for strangers to trust one another without needing a bank or a government as an intermediary, you'd tackle one of society's biggest bottlenecks. But in order to do so, you'd need a powerful system for creating consensus between strangers, and the creators of blockchain believe that power lies in decentralization.Basically all applications of blockchain (and other cryptographic technologies) are based around the concept of decentralization. Instead of a rigid, slow central authority making decisions and governing relationships, blockchain seeks to return regulatory power back to the individuals. Instead of trusting a major institution, blockchain builds trust through consensus.

A NEW TECHNOLOGICAL PARADIGM

The foundation of all blockchain and cryptographic technology is the peer-to-peer network.Traditionally, when we think about trust we think of institutions as the middleman. Right now, if I wanted to send you $100, we'd need to use a bank transfer:

1. First, I'd submit the transfer to the bank.
2. Next, my bank would take a percentage fee to process the transaction
3. My bank verifies that I have $100 in my account
4. My bank asks your bank if your account is valid and open for deposits
5. My bank updates its ledger of accounts to subtract $100 from my account
6. Your bank updates its ledger to add $100 to your account.

A peer-to-peer network doesn't require a middleman. Instead, it uses a distributed ledger to process transactions. Everyone computer that is a part of the network maintains a copy of the ledger, and transactions get added to the ledger systematically. It's incredibly hard to change the ledger once it's written, because that would require changing the copy of the ledger on thousands of computers across the peer-to-peer network.`Here's how the same $100 transfer would work on a peer-to-peer network with a distributed ledger:

1. First, I submit the transfer request to the network
2. Next, the computers nearest to me on the network verify that I have enough currency in my account and that your receiving account is valid
3. Once they verify the transaction, they broadcast the transaction to all the computers near them on the network
4. In turn, those computers re-verify the transaction and pass it along, leading to a waterfall effect until the transaction is now added to every ledger in the peer-to-peer network.

Since the computers on the peer-to-peer network are both users and verifiers, blockchain transactions have the potential to be costless. The waterfall effect of verifying transactions means that a transaction can be processed in minutes or hours, instead of days.

Based on these benefits alone, blockchain is

often touted as the end of institutions. Imagine fast, frictionless transactions to anyone in the world. It's not hard to see the potential advantages, but blockchain presents opportunities for even greater societal changes.

BUILD TRUST

The peer-to-peer nature of blockchain builds trust without institutions. Since everyone who uses the network has a copy of the ledger, blockchain promises a new era of transparency in accounting. I can easily see if you sent me $100 and that the transaction was verified. Once you do, I know you won't be able to rescind the transaction or cancel the charge, because it has been verified by the network.New advances in blockchain also mean that I can create a contract between us that only pays once certain conditions are met, allowing us to do business knowing that the contract is funded and will pay out only if the work is completed.

INCREASE CONNECTION

One of the biggest potential benefits of blockchain technology is increased global connection. When you can easily send currency to anyone in the world, national and regional borders start to break down. It becomes easier to trust strangers, wherever they are in the world. In the same way the internet connected the world, blockchain now promises to create trust between people in the world.But peer-to-peer, blockchain-secured networks aren't just for financial transactions. Blockchain can be used to create contracts between strangers, allow citizens to vote anonymously and end election tampering, and connect smart devices that keep citizens safe. It's even possible blockchain could be used for daily or weekly public referendums on new laws where you could vote from your personal computer. True popular democracy would permanently change the way government functions, giving control of laws and policies to the population.

RAISE PRODUCTIVITY

A second-tier benefit of blockchain is increased productivity. Currently, institutions are a drag on the economy, as governments charge taxes to run the bureaucracy and banks charge fees for transferring and holding money. A blockchain-based economy and society has the potential to be significantly more efficient. As a side effect, the same level of societal trust could be maintained with a significant decrease in the amount of work required.

SECURITY & PRIVACY

So, blockchain has the potential to verify relationships, contracts, and transactions more efficiently than major institutions. But the efficiency is moot if the system is not also highly secure. While peer-to-peer technology has existed since the creation of the internet, these networks weren't secure in the way we expect financial institutions and governments to be.A traditional bank protects privacy by limiting access to information to only the parties involved. Bank ledgers are internal documents, and when you check your transaction history, you can only see the transactions that you're involved in. This role as a trusted third party, maintaining a non-public ledger is the primary role of a bank.Making the ledger public is the foundation of blockchain security, but a public ledger means that privacy is compromised. This was one of the fundamental problems for peer-to-peer transactions prior to 2008. Nobody could figure out how to guarantee privacy while using a publicly-held ledger. The benefits of the distributed ledger were enormous for speed, cost, and reliability. However, consumers weren't likely to adopt a system where all their transactions could be traced.

CRYPTOGRAPHY

The first layer of security and privacy protections on the blockchain is cryptography. Information about transactions is lumped together. This includes transaction ID, time, amount, sender address, and recipient address. The transaction information is then run through a cryptographic hash function before it's added to the ledger. When the transaction information has been encrypted it looks like this (example of a

Bitcoin transaction from October 20, 2017):

aba128d3931e54ce63a69d8c2c1c705ea9f39ca950df136
55d92db662515eacf

A cryptographic hash function shortens and standardizes the number of characters in a transaction description, meaning more transactions can be sent over the network at any time. Just looking at a list of transactions, it's impossible to tell anything about the sender, recipient, and amount. However, since Bitcoin's encryption standards are publicly available is still possible to decrypt the transaction and learn more details, including the sender's public key, the recipient's public key, and the amount sent.

Newer Bitcoin competitors use different types of cryptography to obfuscate the transaction information further, making it impossible to learn information about the transaction once it has been included on the ledger.

We'll discuss encryption and hashing in greater depth in a future chapter.

DISTRIBUTED LEDGER = DIFFICULT TO CHANGE

The distributed ledger, one of the chief challenges for privacy, is also a key to blockchain security.A traditional bank-maintained ledger is protected with many layers of security to prevent unauthorized changes. However, if an attacker was able to access the ledger, they could instantly make changes. Single-owner ledgers are also subject to fraudulent transactions. If an identity thief or malicious vendor sent a transaction request to the bank in your name, it's possible the transaction could be approved without your knowledge. Having a single owner of the ledger means that banks have to spend significant energy and overhead costs on mediating complaints and acting on cases of fraud.The distributed ledger changes these problems. Since thousands of independent copies of the ledger exist on the individual computers in the network, once a transaction has been added to the ledger, it's nearly impossible to change. (We'll discuss the technical reasons why that's the case in a later chapter).

ANONYMITY & PRIVATE KEYS

Since blockchain technology uses a distributed ledger, everyone has a copy of all the transactions that go on in the network. The transaction ledger needs to be public in order to work. However, without proper security measures, anyone in the world could see what you've purchased and from whom.Blockchain implementations solve this security problem in different ways, but most rely on a system that disconnects your personal information from your account. For example, Bitcoin wallets are anonymous, and you can have more than one. The only thing required to access your account is a private key that only you know. While anyone can see your public wallet address, they won't know anything about who the wallet belongs to. In the original white paper for Bitcoin, it's suggested that you create a new wallet for every transaction you conduct on the Bitcoin network in order to maintain anonymity.Other cryptocurrencies, like Monero, hope to further advance the level of privacy for blockchain transactions. Monero uses stealth addresses, decouples user IDs from transaction amounts, and obfuscates transaction trails in order to guarantee privacy (see the chapter on Monero for more information). The result is a completely untraceable cryptocurrency that's still supported by a distributed, public ledger.

IMAGINING A BLOCKCHAIN FUTURE

So far, we've covered the basics of why blockchain was invented, what it does, and a general overview of the methods blockchain uses. We're just scratching the surface, however, and we'll get into the technical details of blockchain solutions in the next chapter.First, though, let's take a look at some potential use cases for blockchain technology. It's important to realize that blockchain technology is much bigger than just Bitcoin. Even if Bitcoin fails tomorrow, blockchain technology will still be viable across many industries.As new development continues into peer-to-peer networking, blockchain programming, and new forms of cryptography, the trend toward distributed trust will continue because of the obvious benefits in terms of speed, cost, and security. While it may not be Bitcoin or Ethereum that powers the future of blockchain, you can be sure that the technologies behind blockchain will get implemented over the course of the next few decades. The overall effect will be more efficient contracts, faster transactions, and lower costs for operators. Blockchain also has the potential to change the way we shop, travel, elect leaders, work, and live.

FINANCE

The financial applications of blockchain get most of the coverage in the media and are usually the first blockchain-based platforms that consumers hear about. Chances are your first exposure to the word "blockchain" was through a discussion about Bitcoin.This makes sense for two reasons. First, the blockchain uses ledgers, and ledgers are best suited to the financial world. The technology is perfectfor financial applications. Second, the first successful blockchain implementation, Bitcoin, was designed from the ground up to be a currency.A blockchain-based financial future looks radically different from the current banking system. The use of cash is already in decline (https://accntu.re/2CnfOnG), and it's likely that western countries could easily transition to all-electronic banking in the near future. In the blockchain future, all transactions could be paid from your cryptocurrency wallet. New, highly scalable technology means your transaction could be processed and verified in seconds. Vendors wouldn't have to pay for payment processing, and purchasing something would likely be as simple as authorizing the transaction using your phone or another connected device.Although a cashless future seems likely, it's not clear who will control the digital currency. Whether decentralized currencies like Bitcoin or major banks will win out in the end is a matter still up for debate. Banks are already considering ways to integrate blockchain technology into their current practices in an attempt to capture the upside of blockchain while still maintaining their role as a trusted middleman in financial transactions.Regulation of financial markets will change as well. Governments need to collect taxes and combat money laundering, and both of those tasks get easier and harder using blockchain. Since the ledger is public, tracking transactions is significantly easier, but with anonymous transactions and shadow accounts, it's likely government financial regulation will get harder. This is one reason why big banks may continue to control financial markets, even after implementing blockchain's best practices.

CONTRACTS

Payments are one example of a blockchain-based contract, but there are already many applications being developed on the blockchain. These contracts use the distributed nature of the blockchain to create trust without needing an institution, and they can't be taken down or disrupted by outside entities.Ethereum is the blockchain where most of these apps are being built, and it's the second most valuable blockchain in the world, after Bitcoin. Ethereum allows developers to build on top of its blockchain, and developers can create programs on Ethereum like they would in any other programming language. This means that Ethereum hosts online games, social media platforms, and service providers just like on the internet. The only difference is that these programs are decentralized. Once created, they will last for as long as the Ethereum blockchain does. Since users around the world sustain the Ethereum blockchain, a government can't have the service taken down, and no one user can delete or alter the service's contents.The cool thing about smart contracts is they're limitless. Anything you can code on a computer can be coded on the blockchain. In the future, this will probably also include artificial intelligence and other forms of machine learning, making AI readily available to anyone who is a part of the blockchain's peer-to-peer network.

GOVERNANCE

Blockchain technology isn't limited to finance. In recent years, technologies have emerged that allow developers to create programs on top of the blockchain. This means that a piece of code is embedded in the blockchain and enforced by the peer-to-peer network. One great example of how this could work is voting.Right now, we rely on elections commissions, central institutions, to administer elections and tally votes. These systems aren't perfect. They require going to the voting station on a certain day in person, verifying your identity and eligibility to vote, and completing a secret ballot in a booth. Each of these steps introduces problems for voters. If I'm unable to get to the voting station on the day in question, I can't vote. If I don't have my identification with me or I haven't been issued a state ID, I can't vote. If I complete my ballot incorrectly, my vote won't be counted, and in some scenarios, technical glitches or miscounting means votes get excluded. At the end of election day, I have to trust the election workers across the country to not cheat and tally the votes fairly. In countries where a dictator is in power or institutions are not strong, elections can be rigged with no recourse for the voters.Blockchain developers hope to solve these problems with smart voting contracts via a distributed ledger on the blockchain. The idea is simple: create a peer-to-peer network where individuals can submit their votes without needing to trust the elections commission or be there in person. However, the implementation is difficult. How do you verify identity? How do you keep people from voting more than once? If the ledger is on the blockchain, how do you keep votes anonymous?It will take some smart cryptography before we have blockchain-based voting, but the implications are enormous. As soon as voting becomes as easy as logging in on your phone or computer and casting your vote, direct democracy and frequent public referendums become more feasible. Policy decisions could be made by the masses. In fact, you could vote on referendums in your city multiple times per day.

While it will take work to make sure that experts are writing and reviewing the policies the public votes on, it's not a far stretch to think governance could become more nimble and responsive thanks to blockchain.

CROWDFUNDING & ICOS

One example of a service using smart contracts is crowdfunding. We're used to thinking about Kickstarter campaigns, and the idea is fairly straightforward. People contribute to a good idea. When the idea reaches its funding goal, the idea's creators get paid to product the idea. If they don't hit the funding goal, the original backers receive their money back.

On the blockchain, all of the fundraising, calculating, and funding/returning money is automated and immutable in a smart contract. As a decentralized app on the blockchain, there's no Kickstarter as a middleman anymore. Instead, the smart contract decides when an idea will be funded, and creators don't pay any fees for the service.Recently, blockchain crowdfunding has grown in popularity for funding new startup ideas, threatening the traditional model of seed funding, venture capital, and institutional investors. Startup founders can now offer a type of public investment vehicle, known as an initial coin offering (ICO), where anyone can invest in an idea in exchange for a stake in the company's growth. While ICOs have become incredibly popular, and many have been successful, they're also largely unregulated, making them very risky investments and subject to questionable investment practices like pump and dump price manipulation.

INSURANCE

Another example of a potential smart contract is car insurance. With the growth of tiny sensors and devices in our cars, we're not far from your car being able to sense when you've been in an accident and send that information to a decentralized application on the blockchain. When integrated with artificial intelligence, computer vision, and smart sensors in your car, the blockchain app could make a decision if you were at fault and pay the claim in seconds, as long as you've been paying your premiums every month. Now, there is no more insurance company for overhead, and the blockchain insurance application doesn't try to make money, so your monthly premiums are only what they need to be.

IDENTITY & IDENTITY OF THINGS
Blockchain's distributed ledger can also host information about identity.

Instead of relying on centralized institutions to issue national IDs, driver's licenses, passports, certificates, diplomas, and accounts, blockchain can facilitate all-in-one seamless identity. Blockchain's security would mean that your transactions remain anonymous by default. However, you could choose to share identity information as part of the fulfillment of a smart contract. Over time, we could standardize global identity and citizenship on the blockchain for every living person.

The same identity management can apply to products, packages, machines, and more. This is called identity of things (IDoT), and it has enormous implications for supply chain management, shipping logistics, infrastructure, and countless other daily interactions. Imagine ordering custom eyeglasses. At the factory, your glasses receive a unique identifier, and you can track the machine ID that is currently working on your glasses ID. Once on it's way, you can track the package ID, knowing where it is, the ID of the truck it's on, and where that truck is currently located.

INTERNET OF THINGS

There are billions of devices in the world that are collecting information every second. Temperature sensors, cameras, and weight scales are all rapidly integrating online. This is the internet of things (IoT).

Traffic lights now use a combination of weight sensors and traffic cameras, along with optimization software, to ease congestion in city centers. Farmers use rain gauges and soil monitoring stations to precisely spread irrigation and fertilizer.

All these billions of devices need a way to store and share their information, and the distributed ledgers are well-suited to these applications. In addition, these devices could learn to trade storage, bandwidth, and processing power in a microeconomy unlike anything we've ever seen before.

How Does the Blockchain Work?

In simplest terms, blockchain uses a combination of cryptography and a public ledger to create trust between parties while maintaining privacy

Understanding the mechanics of how this works is a little bit more difficult, but in order to fully appreciate the genius behind blockchain technology we'll need to dive into the technical details.

While blockchains can include many more features, the fundamentals of a blockchain are in the technology's name:

- The block - A block is a list of transactions from a certain time period. It contains all the information processed on the network within the past few minutes.
- The chain - Each block is timestamped, placed in chronological order, and linked to the block before it using cryptographic algorithms. These algorithms are difficult for computers to calculate and often take several minutes for the fastest computers in the world to solve. Once solved, the cryptographic chain locks the block into place, making it difficult to change. (We'll look at this in greater depth in just a minute).

The chain grows longer over time. Once a new block is created, the computers on the network work together to verify the transactions in the block and secure that block's place in the chain.

In this chapter, we'll take a look at what's inside of a block and how one gets created. We'll then turn to the chain and examine the different ways today's blockchains are secured. We'll try to avoid computer code and complicated explanations. The important thing here is getting a basic understanding of how the parts of a blockchain work together.

DISTRIBUTED LEDGERS

The most fundamental part of the blockchain is the ledger. It's where information about the accounts on the network is stored. The ledger inside the blockchain is what replaces the ledger at a bank or other institution. For a cryptocurrency, this ledger usually consists of account numbers, transactions, and balances. When you submit a transaction to the blockchain, you're adding information to the ledger about where currency is coming from and going to.

As we've already seen, a blockchain ledger is distributed across the network. Every node on the network keeps its own copy of the ledger and updates it when someone submits a new transaction. This "distributed ledger" is how blockchain intends to replace banks and other institutions. Instead of having the bank keep one official copy of the ledger, we'll have everyone keep their own copy of the ledger and then we'll verify transactions by consensus.

Each blockchain technology has its own ledger, and the various ledgers work very differently (as we'll see). However the Bitcoin ledger, the first blockchain ledger, requires three pieces of information to list a transaction:

- An input - If Amy wants to send Ben a Bitcoin, she needs to tell the network where she got that Bitcoin in the first place. Maybe Amy received the Bitcoin yesterday from Sarah, so the first part of the ledger entry says so
- An amount - This is how much Amy wants to send to Ben;
- An output - This is Ben's Bitcoin address where the Bitcoin should be deposited

Now comes a difficult-to-grasp concept: there is no such thing as a Bitcoin. Of course, there are no physical Bitcoins. You probably already knew that. However, there are also no Bitcoins on a hard drive somewhere.

You can't point to a physical object, digital file, or piece of code and say, "this is a Bitcoin." Instead, the entire Bitcoin network is only a series of transaction records. Every transaction in the history of Bitcoin lives in the Bitcoin blockchain's distributed ledger. If you want to prove that you have 20 Bitcoins, the only way you can do it is by pointing to the transactions where you received those 20 Bitcoins.

Almost all blockchains have this characteristic in common. The transaction history is the currency, there's no difference between the two. Some new cryptocurrencies are altering the way the ledger is written in order to provide greater anonymity and privacy in transactions. They use certain identity masking techniques to hide the sender and receiver of the transaction while still maintaining a functional distributed ledger. (We'll look at this in greater depth in the chapters on Dash, Zcash, and Monero.)

THE "DOUBLE SPEND" PROBLEM

Of course, since there is no such thing as a physical cryptocurrency or even a digital file you can point to, we run into a few technical challenges implementing a digital currency. The biggest of these challenges is the double spend problem, where an attacker could send you a token and then send someone else the same token a moment later. Double spend means that tokens could be spent multiple times, increasing inflation and devaluing the cryptocurrency.

When you send a transaction on the Bitcoin blockchain, for instance, you're merely forwarding a transaction you received from someone else. The double spend problem comes when an attacker tries to send a transaction twice, so it works like this:

- The attacker receives Bitcoin from Alice
- The attacker's wallet looks like this: [Alice -> 1BTC -> Attacker] & [Bob -> 1 BTC -> Attacker]
- The attacker then spends the money by forwarding a past transaction. For instance, [Alice > Attacker > You]
- The double spend problem comes when the attacker simultaneously spends the coin twice. For example: [Alice > Attacker > You, 1 BTC] AND [Alice > Attacker > Someone Else, 1 BTC] right after each other.

When you use a bank, the bank would catch this error and invalidate one of the transactions. However, Bitcoin doesn't have a central authority. Instead, Bitcoin uses cryptography to make it statistically very difficult to create false transactions.

First, the attacker could not double spend at the same instant. If he sent two conflicting transactions at the same time, everyone on the network would be able to see both those transactions in the same block. The network would invalidate one.

The attacker could try double spending one right after the other. However, the network would also reject a transaction that references an already-spent coin.

The attacker's only chance is to convince part of the network to accept one of his transactions and convince the other part of the network to accept the

35

other transaction. This splits the network into two streams, called "forks." Multiple forks of the blockchain can exist on Bitcoin.

The creators of Bitcoin solved this forking challenge, and double spend problem, by making the link between blocks difficult to compute. Since it takes so long to cryptographically create and validate a new block, it's unlikely two blocks will be created at the same time. Even if two blocks are created simultaneously, the Bitcoin protocol directs participants in the network to follow the longest chain. As soon as a new block is created the network will revert back to a single version of the ledger.

Since multiple forks are theoretically possible, it's wise to wait for multiple blocks to go by before considering a transaction "confirmed." Once confirmed, however, that transaction is immutable. It's nearly impossible to create a fraudulent blockchain fast enough to replace the honest blockchain. Let's dive into how it works.

CREATING A BLOCK

The distributed ledger is the core of the block, but it's not the only thing that goes into a newly created block. There is a header and a footer required for every block. Additionally, the transactions included in the block are put through a process that compresses, encodes, and standardizes them. When a verifier creates a new block, it looks completely different from the ledger it was based off of. However, the underlying ledger is still there and can be verified in the future when new transactions require information about the previous blocks.Not every computer on the blockchain network will work on creating and encrypting blocks. Those tasks are generally left up to a specific group of verifiers who choose to review the transactions in the block in exchange for a reward. There are several ways these verifiers review, validate, and certify the transactions in a block. We'll look at those validation methods in the sections about "proof of work" and "proof of stake".Before they reach the point of certifying the block's contents, they have to create the block. No matter the blockchain, block creation generally follows a similar procedure:

- ☐ Add new transactions
- ☐ Compile and shorten the ledger
- ☐ Stamp it with the time and block ID.

Let's take a look at how that all works together.

ADDING TRANSACTIONS

The first step in building a block is gathering and adding all the current transactions to the block's ledger. When a user creates a new transaction, they broadcast that transaction to the entire network. As a verifier, your computer's job is to review the transaction to make sure it's valid. Since blockchain currencies are nothing more than a series of transactions, your first step to verify a transaction is to look at where the sender says they originally got their funds. Verifiers keep a complete history of the entire blockchain, back to the very first block. They have a record of every transaction that has ever happened on the network.

As a verifier, you review the history of the blockchain to find the block and transaction where the sender received the funds. If that input transaction is confirmed on the blockchain, then the transaction is valid and you'll need to confirm the receiving party's address. If the input transaction doesn't exist or has already been spent, then the current transaction is invalid, and it won't be included in the ledger. As the verifier, it's your job to include and verify as many transactions in the past few minutes as possible. For instance, on the Bitcoin blockchain, a new block is created every ten minutes, on average. With every new block, the Bitcoin blockchain adds 1,500 to 2,000 new transactions. That's over 200,000 transactions per day, and each one has to be verified.

Verifiers are said to be operating "full nodes." A node is a point on the peer-to-peer network. It's a full node because the verifier has downloaded the full history of the blockchain and is verifying transaction requests on the network.

COMPILING THE LEDGER

Once you've verified all the transactions in your block, it's time to create the ledger. For a simple example, you'll start by listing the transactions one right after another:

```
[Input Address][Sender's Address][Amount][Output
address],

[Input Address][Sender's Address][Amount][Output
address],

[Input Address][Sender's Address][Amount][Output
address],

[Input Address][Sender's Address][Amount][Output
address], ...
```

Then you'll apply a cryptographic technique called hashing to each of the transactions. At its most basic, hashing takes a string of characters and generates another string of characters. So, when you feed the input, amount, and output address to a hashing algorithm it will turn the transaction into a string of characters unique to that transaction, like this:

```
aba128d3931e54ce63a69d8c2c1c705ea9f39ca950d
f13655d92db662515eacf
```

```
-This is an actual transaction hash from
the Bitcoin blockchain
```

We've seen this example before in the "cryptography & security" section of the first chapter. But now let's dig into what hashing accomplishes:

- It standardizes - You could have transactions of different sizes and complexity and they'd all get changed into a string of 64 characters. Whether it's one word or a whole paragraph, any text could be standardized to a 64 character hash.
- It's unique - The way the cryptographic algorithm works, changing even one character of the original text gives you a completely different output.
- It's deterministic - As long as you enter the exact same original input, you will always get the same output.
- It works in only one way - This is called pre-image resistance. The output of a hash is directly tied to the input, but it would be incredibly difficult to work backwards and figure out the input given only the output.

Here's an example of hashing in action to illustrate these concepts:

Input	Output
Hello	185f8db32271fe25f561a6fc938b2e264306ec304eda518007d1764826381969
Hello.	2d8bd7d9bb5f85ba643f0110d50cb506a1fe43e769a22503193ea6046bb87f7
hello	2cf24dba5fb0a30e26e83b2ac5b9e29e1b161e5c1fa7425e73043362938b9824

You can see that even the tiniest change in the input yields a completely different output (unique), and no matter the length of the input text, I'll always receive a 64 character (in this hashing function) output text (standardized). It's not random because I will always get the same hash from inputting "Hello" (deterministic), but if I gave you the output, it would be very difficult to work backwards to find the input (pre-image resistance).

So, we use hashing to standardize data while making sure that it hasn't been tampered with. If someone were to try to change a transaction in the blockchain, they'd have to rehash that transaction, and it would look entirely different. It would be obvious that it had been tampered with.

To make it even more difficult to tamper with the blockchain and reduce memory required to store the transaction ledger, most blockchains hash more than once. This means that they take the hash of a transaction, combine it with a hash of another transaction, and re-hash that into a new smaller hash. Combining transactions in this way is known as a Merkle Tree, and the root hash of all the transactions is included at the beginning of the block. Understanding why we need a Merkle Tree is a topic for a more in-depth book, but on a basic level the Merkle Tree shows that all the transactions in the block are valid while using less memory in the long run.

TIME STAMP & BLOCK ID

The final element in a block is the time stamp and any block ID information. This makes it easy to look up previous blocks once time has gone by. Future transactions will also be able to point to this block ID as the block containing the input transaction (also known as the "coinbase") for the current transaction.

LINKING BLOCKS TOGETHER

The final step of creating a block is linking it to the previous blocks in the chain. There are a few ways to do this, but virtually all of them involve hashing in some way to make the content of the previous block part of the new block.Remember that hashing takes an input, no matter how big or small, and turns it into a string of characters. If you change the input even slightly, the entire output gets changed. In order to include the previous block's contents in the new block, we can take the hash of the entire previous block and add that to the beginning of the next block. Doing so means that we've effectively linked the old block to the new block, because if anything changes in the older block, even the tiniest change, the entire block's hash will change.Now, once a block has been completed it becomes MUCH harder to change it. Making an edit to an older block means you'd have to re-hash that entire block. Once you re-hash all of block 1, you'd have to crack open block 2, delete block 1's old hash, insert block 1's new hash, and now re-hash all of block 2. But new blocks are being created all the time, so in order to change an older transaction, you'd have to edit every block after that transaction took place. The more time that goes by, the harder it becomes to hack the network and successfully change a transaction. Hashing is at the core of blockchain security. The cryptography makes the transaction ledger difficult to change, meaning the ledger can be public and secure at the same time.However, the hashing itself is not that difficult. Most computers could easily re-hash a blockchain in a few seconds. So, in order to guarantee the hashing security does its job, we need to introduce a level of difficulty to the creation of a new block. Ideally, it would be something that slows an attacker down and makes it more likely that honest members of the network will win. In the Bitcoin blockchain (and most other modern blockchains) that added difficulty is called "proof of work".

PROOF OF WORK

In order to slow down attackers and guarantee blockchain security, there needs to be more honest verifiers on the network than dishonest attackers. In other words, since the blockchain is based on consensus, we need a system where people are rewarded for being honest and punished for creating false transactions. We also need to slow down block creation so that the whole network has a chance to verify transactions and certify new blocks before the next block is created.

The most widely adopted solution to this problem is proof of work. At its simplest, the proof of work system involves giving all the computers on the network a very difficult problem. The computers who choose to compete to solve this problem are called miners. After each miner compiles the current block, they'll begin the process of solving the difficult puzzle for that block. The first computer on the network to solve the puzzle receives a prize, and the block that computer compiled is accepted across the network as the new block in the chain.

The prize for solving the puzzle is called a "block reward," and it's an incentive for new miners to join the network and try to work on the newest block. Currently (Feb 12, 2018), the Bitcoin block reward is 12.5 BTC or $108,000 USD. If your computer solves the puzzle, you get that reward. Needless to say, there are now tens of thousands of miners on the Bitcoin network, all fighting to solve the puzzle and earn the reward. The result is the Bitcoin network has far-reaching independent verification. If you wanted to try to change the Bitcoin blockchain, you'd need more computing power than those tens of thousands of miners combined.

So, what is this puzzle that's at the core of Bitcoin's security?

MINING

The fundamental characteristic of the puzzle is you can't find the answer without repeated guess-and-check. Solving the puzzle and winning the block reward doesn't require any special skills or hardware. It just takes time. In fact, your home computer or mobile phone could complete the puzzle given enough time.

Since the puzzle requires repeated hammering away until you find the right answer and win the prize, the people who participate in solving these blockchain-based puzzles are called miners.

Mining on Bitcoin or any other proof of work

cryptocurrency involves adding one more piece to the block before it's complete. This little additional piece is called a "nonce," and it's essential to proof of work systems. The nonce is the answer to the puzzle. It's also completely meaningless on its own.Remember we discussed hashing and the way hashing turns an entire block information into a single string of characters. For instance, a hash of a block might look like this:

```
f358f1293d6ed3a3b029af24bd0818c531e8e31caf6
d062577b4f6876e53d650
```

The puzzle behind proof of work is all about using the nonce to manipulate the block's hash. Stay with me here, as this could get confusing, but we'll have an example in a second to clear things up. If we added one letter or number to the above block, we'd get an entirely different hash, like this:

```
eb5c7f52857a294c3f5925b1d66cbf9dd4760ca1f7e
047453636c661fc093e8e
```

So the puzzle behind proof of work is to get the block's hash to start with a zero [0...]. Eventually, if I keep adding nonsense characters onto the end of the block, I'll eventually get a hash that starts with a zero. Once I do, I've solved the problem. The little bit of nonsense characters I had to place at the end? That's the nonce.

Here's an example. Let's just say we're trying to solve a proof of work for the string "Hello". But this time, instead of accepting any nonsense characters, let's say the nonce has to be the lowest number possible. Finding the answer, I'd need to count up from zero until I got a winning answer. It would look like this:

Input	Output
Hello	eb5c7f52857a294c3f5925b1d66cbf9dd4760c a1f7e047453636c661fc093e8e
Hello0	80878c5b013ba72c0d2b7e8f65868649cbdb1e 7e7a8c8a07537d6b3619e4e32f
Hello1	948edbe7ede5aa7423476ae29dcd7d61e7711a 071aea0d83698377effa896525
Hello2	be98c2510e417405647facb89399582fc499c3 de4452b3014857f92e6baad9a9
Hello3	0945f30798c28800c64afeb4bd218873fa7a2a d2e97ee68db067b2eb63cb0e9c

In this example, my output hash started with a zero when my nonce was "3." We didn't have to try too many nonces in order to get the right answer! That was pretty easy. But it would get a lot harder if you asked me to find a nonce that output a hash with two leading zeroes [00...], and I wouldn't want to find the nonce for three leading zeroes [000...] by hand.

The current Bitcoin difficulty is 18 leading zeroes [000000000000000000... - it's a little more complicated than the number of leading zeros, as we'll see in the next chapter, but leading zeros is a good, visual way to understand mining difficulty]. It takes some of the fastest computers in the world around ten minutes to find the right nonce for Bitcoin's mining reward. It's hard to overstate how difficult of a problem Bitcoin miners are solving. We'll dive deeper into difficulty in the next chapter on hashing.

The high reward of mining makes it worth dedicating all that computing power to such a difficult problem for some miners with highly efficient machines. For attackers, the high difficulty level makes it very difficult to submit a bad block to the network, and nearly impossible to change an existing block. In order to do that, you'd need to be able to calculate the new nonce for the block you wanted to change and every block thereafter. And you'd need to be able to do it with more computing power than the honest miners on the network so that your new chain of blocks would grow faster and eventually overtake the honest chain.

(If you want to learn more about mining and the potential to get involved in cryptocurrency mining yourself, check out my Ultimate Guide to Cryptocurrency Mining).

CONSENSUS

When a miner solves the difficult puzzle, the computer broadcasts its answer to the network. Full nodes and other miners on the network review the history of the ledger check the miner's answer to make sure it includes valid transactions.

If it does, then this is the most recent valid block, and other miners will begin working on a new puzzle based on the results of the completed block. If the newly mined block is invalid, the nodes in the network will refuse to accept it. Nobody will start working on a new block atop the invalid block, and so the invalid block will be orphaned.

The miners on the network are programmed to only work on the longest valid chain. In this way, the computing power of the network converges on a single valid chain over time and avoids invalid chains.

THE 51% PROBLEM

In order to implement an attack and create an invalid chain, you would need more computing power than the honest miners on the blockchain. This is called the "51% problem." If, somehow, an attacker were able to amass 51% of the mining power on a blockchain, the attacker could feasibly create phony transactions.

On major blockchains today, a 51% attack is highly unlikely. Established, valuable currencies already have tens of thousands of miners with incredible amounts of computing power. In order to gain 51% of the computing power on the Bitcoin or Ethereum mining network, you'd need to invest millions of dollars in hardware.

The newer, less established blockchain currencies may have less computing power, but they also are less valuable. A 51% attack against these more vulnerable currencies would be less profitable. That's not to mention the fact that attacking the currency would almost certainly cause it to lose value on public exchanges.

COSTS

Proof of work is well proven and effective, but it's not without its problems. The biggest problem is energy consumption. Since hundreds of thousands of computers are working on the same problem, proof of work mining consumes a lot of electricity. Current estimates believe (http://blockgeeks.com/bitcoins-energy-consumption/) that proof of work mining could use as much electricity as the entire country of Denmark by 2020.

The problem with energy consumption is compounded when you consider we pay our electricity bills with fiat currency (e.g. dollars, euros, pounds, yen). This means the cryptocurrency revolution is paradoxically creating a huge need for the currencies it's trying to replace.

PROOF OF STAKE

A small handful of lesser-known coins have led the charge away from proof of work toward another means of verification known as "proof of stake." Their early success and overall interest from developers in exploring less energy-intensive options has led the second biggest cryptocurrency in the world, Ethereum, to seriously consider a switch from proof of work to proof of stake.

The difference between the two systems is huge. Proof of work involves thousands of computers competing to solve a puzzle. In proof of stake, the creator of a new block is chosen based on the percentage of the overall coin supply they own. For example if I own 1% of all Ethereum coins in the world,

I have a 1% chance of being chosen to create the next block.

When it's your turn, you assemble all the transactions and compile the block's pieces. You then link it to the previous block. While there's no "block reward" in proof of stake, you do receive any transaction fees paid for the transactions in that block. After you submit the block to the network for approval, someone else will get chosen to assemble the next block. You won't get to create a block again for a period of time.

If you decide to include fake transactions or alter the transactions in the block you're building, you take a huge risk. If the network catches you, you'll forfeit all of your coins. In this way, you earn a small reward for being honest, and you stand to lose everything if you're dishonest.

ENERGY SAVINGS

Since only one computer on the network has to work to build the block at a time, the energy savings are enormous. Remember that with proof of work, thousands of computers are competing on the same problem, but only one of them wins. This means that all the other non-winners just wasted the electricity they spent on the problem. Proof of stake, on the other hand, has the potential to be thousands of times more cost effective compared to proof of work.

Proof of stake still requires other computers on the network to verify transactions and review the work of the current block builder, but those computers don't need to run their processors at max capacity (as in proof of work) in order to do their job.

FUTURE

Proof of stake is still a small technology, and it hasn't yet been adopted by any of the major players in cryptocurrency. However, that's about to change in 2018 when Ethereum plans to implement a change from proof of work to proof of stake. Ethereum's switch will be the first large-scale adoption of the new proof of stake protocol. In all likelihood, the switch will involve a "hard fork." This means that an older version of the Ethereum blockchain will continue to exist with proof of work, but the new currency will branch off and compete with its legacy brother. If Ethereum successfully implements proof of stake, it could be the first of many currencies making the change.

OTHER CONSENSUS MECHANISMS

There are many other consensus mechanisms, including proof of activity, proof of burn, proof of capacity, byzantine fault tolerance-based methods, and others. Each of these makes up a small portion of blockchain projects and is too detailed to explore in-depth in this book. As someone new to blockchain, you should know about proof of work and proof of stake, but also know that new consensus methods are out there and on the rise as proof of work reaches its limits.

CRYPTOGRAPHIC HASH FUNCTIONS: A DEEP DIVE ON HOW BLOCKCHAIN HASHING WORKS

This chapter is here by popular demand from reader comments. It's a deep dive into how hashing works. This is going to get very technical, and you don't have to read this section in order to understand the basics of blockchain. Feel free to skip to the next chapter, "Bitcoin: The Mother of All Blockchain," if this chapter gets too technical for you. You'll still be able to understand the rest of the book without reading this chapter. For those brave souls who want to dive into hashing, let's get started.

WHAT IS A CRYPTOGRAPHIC HASH FUNCTION?

Bitcoin mining, and other proof of work schemes, use cryptographic hash functions extensively. So, anyone who wants to deeply understand blockchain needs to learn about cryptographic hashing.

We already know that a cryptographic hash function takes a string of characters, no matter how long, and transforms that string to a string of random characters of a standard length. (In the example we'll be using, the output is 64 characters in length, but there are longer and shorter hashing functions.)

We saw earlier that a hash function has a few core properties:

1. It's a one-way functions, meaning:
   a. It's easy to work forward to calculate the hash of an input (maybe not easy by hand, as we'll see, but easy for a computer).
   b. It's infeasible to work backwards to find an input that produces a given hash. (a.k.a. pre-image resistance). The only way to do this is brute force, guessing and checking potential inputs thousands or millions of times.
2. A small change to an input changes its hash value dramatically.
3. It's deterministic, so the same input always produces the same hash.

These properties make hashing an ideal solution for all kinds of applications, not just for blockchain. You can use a hash function to add a digital signature to a document. If you post the document's hash online along with a file, anyone who downloads the file can quickly see if it has been modified or tampered with, just by running a hash and comparing it with the one you posted online.

You can also use the hash of a file or document as that document's unique ID. For the algorithm we'll look at in this chapter, SHA-256, there has never been an instance where two different inputs have produced the same output. (This is called "collision" in cryptography.) There are 2^{256} possible hash outputs. Even the most powerful computers in the world working together would need more time than the entire history of the universe in order to find a SHA-256 collision.

HASHING HISTORY

SHA stands for "Secure Hash Algorithm." The SHA cryptographic hash algorithms are the most widely used and recognized. They come from the United States' National Security Agency, an intelligence agency that's responsible for signals intelligence, transmitting and intercepting foreign intelligence and counterintelligence.

The NSA shared the SHA algorithms publicly because, even knowing how they work, you can't subvert or deconstruct them. SHA is now standardized and maintained by the National Institute for Standards and Technology.

There are other hash algorithms in use in a variety of projects. This chapter will focus on SHA, specifically SHA-256, but it's worth noting that blockchains can and do run on a variety of hash algorithms. They accomplish similar goals but require different hardware to run efficiently, hence the variation.

HIGH-LEVEL OVERVIEW OF HASHING IN PROOF-OF-WORK

For our purposes, hash algorithms are useful for proof-of-work mining, as described above. Miners compile all the block's information. Then, they append a nonce to the block's header. They start by appending zero,

"0000000000"

And they complete a SHA-256 hash of the block. The result looks like this:

"8fc49a37693b9427e0dfd4d09d03faf974fe82701a 2f1c1ee078924f87507166"

Remember, mining on Bitcoin is only successful when you find a hash that has 18 leading zeroes. This is an unsuccessful hash, so we'll need to try another nonce.

Due to the characteristics of hashing algorithms, trying a slightly different nonce will give us a completely different answer.

However, Bitcoin rewards the miner who finds the lowest nonce, so we'll iterate by one and try again:

Nonce: "0000000001"

Hash:
"d13b969ce6872745059bf8516211d49b904d0b5fcd
e9b11b8195235b7ee6ce38"

Still no luck. Let's keep trying, iterating through nonces from 0 to 9,999,999,999. At some point, we may find one that has a hash with 18 leading zeroes:

"000000000000000000005ef2bdc34baac64d1f51e209
554202c83fad1f857619d1"

If so, congratulations! We've just mined our first successful Bitcoin block. We'll broadcast the block out to the network. Everyone will run our block and our nonce, and if they agree that the block is valid, we'll get the block reward. In fact, we've already included a transaction in our block that sends us 12.5 newly-mined BTC. Once we find a block, everyone starts on mining a new block and the process starts over.

It's highly unlikely we'll find a successful hash, though. It's probable that we'll get to a nonce of "9999999999" and none of our hashes will have met the criteria (18 zeroes). What can we do?

Well, chances are time has gone by since we started checking nonces. We can update the timestamp in our block. Since even a small change to the block means the hash will be entirely different, we can now work through 0 to 9,999,999,999 again. We can also change the order of transactions in our block, add more transactions, or modify the address for the 12.5 BTC mining reward (the coinbase transaction) to go to.

All of these small changes introduce 9,999,999,999 more possible nonces we need to check, until we find one with 18 leading zeroes. That may seem like a lot, but consider that the fastest mining computers can compute over 1 terahashes per second. That's 1,000,000,000,000 attempts every second. All the mining computers on the Bitcoin network have a combined hashrate of over 22,000,000,000,000,000,000 hashes per second. Still, at the current difficulty (18 zeroes) it takes all those computers ten minutes, on average, to find a successful hash.

It's hard to overstate how difficult it is to find a successful hash. It's harder than trying to locate a single grain of sand in all the world's beaches. This is the key to proof-of-work security. Overwriting the blockchain with a fraudulent chain would require you to hash faster than the nodes on the honest chain. That's extremely improbable.

DOES HASHING APPLY IN PROOF OF STAKE AND OTHER CONSENSUS MECHANISMS?

Yes! Proof of stake systems and many other consensus mechanisms still rely on hashing, although the difficulty requirements and ability to modify the hash of a given block are greatly changed. These consensus mechanisms do not rely on hashing alone to secure the blockchain like proof of work does.

That said, hashing still links blocks together and serves as a signature that the block has not been modified. We also use hashing to create new wallet addresses and in various other locations throughout blockchain applications.

A Quick Word About Proof of Work Mining Difficulty

I've been defining mining difficulty by the number of leading zeroes a successful hash needs to have, since it's an easy visual way to understand mining difficulty. The truth is more complicated and variable.

Bitcoin adjusts the difficulty of mining a new block based on how much hashing power is currently on its network. As more miners join, Bitcoin adjusts the mining to become more difficult. These adjustments are not set in terms of leading zeroes. Instead, they're updated as a formula. The block's hash needs to be less than the target difficulty.

In practice, this means that hash may need to be less than 18 zeroes AND something else, like this:

```
New hash < 00000000000000000075
```

You could theoretically hash a block that has 18 leading zeroes, but it would still fail to be valid if the nest digits were higher than "75."

Therefore, Bitcoin's difficulty adjustments are much finer tuned than just adding or subtracting zeroes from the beginning of the   hash.

So, we've seen how difficult it is to find a successful nonce and mine a Bitcoin block. But what exactly is the computer's processor doing when it completes the SHA-256 hash?

This is the part where things get very nerdy very quickly. Reader, beware. We're going to walk through an example of a successful SHA-256 hash to mine a Bitcoin block to see exactly how it works. Basically, we're going to mine a Bitcoin block by hand, right now, right here in this book.

High-Level Look at Bitcoin Mining

Bitcoin mining takes a 160 character input (known as a "block header") and hashes it to a 64 character output (the block's hash). As we've discussed, at the current difficulty, the first 18 characters of the block's hash must be zero in order for the block to be successfully mined.

We accomplish this in two rounds of SHA-256, but functionally they're carried out like three rounds.

Round 1.1 hashes the first 128 characters of the block header. This is the limit of SHA-256.

Round 1.2 hashes characters 129-160 followed by zeroes that pad the message and fill the second round (more on this in a minute).

Round 2 combines the outputs of Round 1.1 and 1.2 and re-hashes them to produce a final hash value. The result of round two is the block's hash.

Prepare Your Header Fields
The first step to mining a block is to prepare the ledger of transactions that will go into your block.

As we mentioned earlier, transactions get paired up and hashed together in rounds of hashing known as a Merkle Tree. We won't demonstrate a Merkle Tree here, but the result of a Merkle Tree is a unique Merkle Root hash for all the transactions in the block. A Merkle Root looks like this:

"2E99F445C007A9158207CC30CEBAD2B3D26C45FDAB 2EBDF50D261335FC00D92C"

Once we have our Merkle Root, we can prepare the necessary elements that go into a block header:

- **The Version**: Bitcoin is currently Version 2

- **The Previous Block's Hash:** "00000000000000000A2940884E0C3BC96510 CAD11912A527E9D15DF42F0E1D67" (Notice the leading zeroes that indicate this was a successful previous block. This example has only 17 leading zeroes, because I am using a block from 2014 [block #334592] where someone else has already done the math by hand. Bitcoin mining has gotten more difficult since then.)
- **Merkle Root:** "2E99F445C007A9158207CC30CEBAD2B3D26C 45FDAB2EBDF50D261335FC00D92C"
- **Time:** Dec 16, 2014 1:05:40 PM
- **Bits:** 404454260 (This is the current difficulty level)
- **Nonce:** 3225483075 (This is a successful nonce)

Now that we have all the necessary pieces, we need to convert them into a standard format. SHA-256 uses base-16 hexadecimal for all numbers. So, we'll convert base-10 digits to base-16, using 0-9 AND a-f to make 16 digits. We'll also need to convert the timestamp to standard Unix time in seconds since 1970-01-01 00:00, and then convert that to hexadecimal as well.

When we're done we get this:

Version	
	00000002
PrevHash	0000000000000000A2940884E0C3BC9651 0CAD11912A527E9D15DF42F0E1D67
MerkleRoot	2E99F445C007A9158207CC30CEBAD2B3D26 C45FDAB2EBDF50D261335FC00D92C
Time	54907474
Bits	181B7B74
Nonce	
	C040F743

Little Endian Conversion

The next step is called little-endian conversion. This has to do with how the individual bytes of data are ordered when we store and process them. I won't bore you with the details and arguments for little-endian vs big-endian. Suffice it to say, we need to change the order of the numbers we're using.

To do so, we need to reverse the order of the bytes of data. Practically this means we'll group the numbers in pairs and reverse the order of the pairings.

```
"C0 40 F7 43" becomes "43 F7 40 C0"
```

After little endian, our data looks like this:

Version	02000000
PrevHash	671D0E2FF45DD1E927A51219D1CA1065C9 3B0C4E8840290A0000000000000000
MerkleRoot	2CD900FC3513260DF5BD2EABFD456CD2B3 D2BACE30CC078215A907C045F4992E
Time	74749054
Bits	747B1B18
Nonce	43F740C0

You can flip the page back to the old data to compare.

Concatenation & Padding
We're now going to combine all our block data together into one string like this:

"02000000671D0E2FF45DD1E927A51219D1CA1065C9
3B0C4E8840290A00000000000000002CD900FC35132

60DF5BD2EABFD456CD2B3D2BACE30CC078215A907C0
45F4992E74749054747B1B1843F740C0"

This is the 160 character block header.

The first 128 characters of this will be our message for round 1.1 of SHA-256:

"02000000671D0E2FF45DD1E927A51219D1CA1065C9
3B0C4E8840290A0000000000000000002CD900FC35132
60DF5BD2EABFD456CD2B3D2BACE30CC078215A907C0
"

The remaining characters need some padding to fill up round 1.2:

"45F4992E74749054747B1B1843F740C0...[need padding here]"

So, we'll put an "8" to mark the end of the message. Then, we'll place a "280" at the end of the string to signal that the message we're hashing is 640 bits long (160 hex characters = 80 bytes = 640 bits; 640 written in hexadecimal is 280)...

"45F4992E74749054747B1B1843F740C0 8 ...
280"

Finally, we'll fill in the remaining space, up to 128 characters, with zeroes for padding.

"45F4992E74749054747B1B1843F740C08000000000
00000000000000000000000000000000000000000000
00000000000000000000000000000000000000000280
"

This is the message for round 1.2 of SHA-256.

Blocking or Chunking
Now, we'll divide the data for round 1.1 into 16 chunks in preparation for hashing.

1. 02000000

2. 671D0E2F

3. F45DD1E9

69

. . .

```
16. 15A907C0
```

This is where the hashing begins. We'll now create 48 more chunks, for a total of 64 chunks.

We create chunks 17-64 by adding together prior chunks along with scrambled bits of prior chunks. Specifically, the formula is:

```
Hashes 17-64 = 16 prior + 7 prior + mix(15
        prior) + mix(2 prior)
```

This creates completely new, unrelated values for chunks 17-64.

Main Hash Algorithm
Now that we have 64 chunks, we're ready for the main hash algorithm. It's complicated, but stay with me.

Defining W & A-H
Our 64 chunks are the message that we'll run through our has algorithm. In the algorithm, the message is variable "w." In our example w_1=02000000, w_2=671D0E24, etc...

The hash algorithm also involves variables A through H. For our first round A-H is provided by the NSA, but they come from a mathematical source, the fractional portion of the first 8 primes:

$$A = sqrt(2) \% 1$$

$$B = sqrt(3) \% 1$$

$$C = sqrt(5) \% 1$$

$$\ldots$$

$$H = sqrt(19) \% 1$$

If that "%" symbol looks unfamiliar in a formula, don't worry. It's called a modulo. It means "give the remainder of division." For example, sqrt(2) = 1.41421356237. Sqrt(2) % 1 = 0.41421356237. Written in hexadecimal, that's 6A09E667, and that's the value the NSA provided for A in our first round of SHA-256. Here's A-H from the NSA (or from the square root of the first 8 primes modulo 1):

$$A = 6A09E667$$

$$B = BB67AE85$$

```
C = 3C6EF372

D = A54FF53A

E = 510E527F

F = 9B05688C

G = 1F83D9AB

H = 5BE0CD19
```

Step 1: Shift A-C & E-H

Step 1 in the main hash algorithm is to shift 6 of the values for A-H. The old value for A becomes the new value for B, like this:

```
Old A -> New B

Old B -> New C

Old C -> New D

(skip the old value for D)

Old E -> New F

Old F -> New G

Old G -> New H

(old H does not        become new A)
```

Now, we have new values for B-D and F-H.

Step 2: Find A & E
We still need to get new values for A and E. To do so, we follow a formula that performs several nonlinear transformations on the data. These formulas are also the first place where the message, variable "w," enters the main hash algorithm.

I'll share the formulas here, but I won't go into detail on how they work, so that I don't bore you to death.

New A =

- w_1 (the first part of the message out of the 64 chunks we created) +
- K_0 (this is a constant from the NSA, and it changes with every iteration of the hash K_0 up to K_{64}) +
- Old H
- Maj(oldABC) (this is a function performed on the 1s and 0s of binary that make up A, B, and C) +
- Choose(oldEFG) (another function on the 1s and 0s, this time of E, F, and G) +
- Sum(A shift 2, 13, & 22)%2 (this also plays with binary, shifting the 1s and

◻ 0s by 2, 13, and 22 places and adding the results, then taking the sum modulo 2 [basically seeing if the sum is even or odd]) +
◻ Sum(E shift 6, 11, & 25)%2 (same thing except with E this time, and different shifts)

Whew, that's exhausting. Add all that up (in hexadecimal, of course), and you have the new value for A. Now, we'll do a similar process for E:

New E =

◻ W_1 +
◻ K_0 +
◻ oldD +
◻ choose(oldEFG) +
◻ sum(E>>6, 11, 25) % 2

Hopefully, you followed along with the above variables and formulas. They're similar to the ones I described for new A. Now, we have new E.

Step 3: Do that 63 more times

At this point, we've completed 1/64 of one round of SHA-256. We'll need to do this whole process 63 more times for all the values w_2 through w_{64}.

Step 4: Add the final result to the NSA's A-H

When we finish, we'll add the new A-H from w_{64} to the original A-H from the NSA. This is step 65, but it's not a hashing, just addition. The resulting A-H is our final SHA-256 hash:

```
New A = 09A0D191

New B = 92EF77C3

New C = 04FE4478

New D = 88F9EF50

New E = 69D64846

New F = 5A19146F

New G = B7706197

New H = 14D08904
```

```
(Amidst all this theory and math, did you
  forget we're actually mining a Bitcoin
```

block here? The values above are the real values for A-H after Round 1.1 of Bitcoin block #334592)

Next Steps

So, we've completed Round 1.1 of hashing, running all 64 chunks (w_1-w_{64}) through SHA-256 and getting a final result.

But wait. We're not done. We haven't done Round 1.2 or Round 2 of hashing yet. Remember our original message was longer than 128 characters, so it didn't all fit in the first round. We have to keep going!

For round 1.2 of SHA-256, we won't use the NSA's A-H. We'll just keep going with the output A-H of round 1.1. From there, the process is exactly the same, including the 64 chunks, the formulas, and adding the results to the original A-H in step 65.

New A = 3EBB2D68

New B = D7007148

New C = B184E57B

New D = BA9697D7

New E = 6BC04141

New F = 155C57F9

New G = 7E3B92C5

New H = FD6A46BD

(The values above are the real values for A-H after Round 1.2 of Bitcoin block #334592)

Now we're ready for Round 2. The output from Round 1.2 (new A-H) is now our message (w_1-w_8). Except the output from 1.2 is only 64 characters long, and we need to input 128 characters into the hash function, so we'll use padding again, adding an 8, many zeros, and "100" at the end this time because our message is 256 bits long (100 in hexadecimal).

For Round 2, the final round, we'll use the NSA constants again for A-H. After that, the 64 steps of hashing and the 65th step of addition are all the same as before. In the end, we get our final hash:

Final A = FF277F1F

Final B = 11CD72EF

```
Final C = FE537F5E

Final D = 8A2690E0

Final E = 8D8C9116

Final F = 82D8A815

Final G = 00000000

Final H = 00000000
```

Put it all together and little endian convert it back for left-to-right reading:

000000000000000015A8D88216918C8DE090268A5E7 F53FEEF72CD111F7F27FF

In December 2014, those 16 leading zeros were enough to satisfy the difficulty level. This was a successfully mined block!

Today, since Bitcoin's difficulty has increased, it would not be. If we got this final hash today, we'd have to start over from the beginning with a new nonce.

BITCOIN: THE MOTHER OF ALL BLOCKCHAIN

Launched in 2009, Bitcoin is the first and most famous blockchain technology. Eight years later, Bitcoin is still the most popular cryptotoken on the market. Recently, interest in Bitcoin has become mainstream with even Wall Street investors considering providing Bitcoin futures investment-grade securities.

While Bitcoin's rise has been meteoric over the past few years, the currency has faced its share of challenges along the way. For the first few years after its inception, Bitcoin faced ridicule in the press for attempting to create a new global currency. Early on, a mysterious security breach meant that millions of dollars worth of Bitcoins went missing. Bitcoin weathered those first few obstacles, but it still faces challenges today.

Some of Bitcoin's current challenges are technical. The original Bitcoin network wasn't built to support the amount of transactions currently taking place. The Bitcoin community is rife with debate about the best course to fix its scalability problem.

Bitcoin's other challenge is economics. Much of Bitcoin's current value is based on speculation. You'd be hard pressed to find grocery stores or coffee shops accepting Bitcoin. The number of businesses accepting Bitcoin grows every year, especially online, but it's still rare to find a company accepting Bitcoin. While Bitcoin has huge potential if it's accepted as a legitimate currency, it's current value is based on potential, not on concrete reality. As a result, many financial experts have called Bitcoin (and other cryptocurrencies) a bubble that's likely to pop soon.

In this chapter, we'll give a brief overview of Bitcoin's history and growth. However, Bitcoin news changes daily, and this isn't a book about investing. If you're thinking about buying Bitcoin, read more than just this book! I explained the basics in my previous book, *Mastering Bitcoin for Starters (amzn.to/2AwSNy0)*. The history and technology are compelling, but you'll need to do more research to decide if Bitcoin is worth its current $8,600 per BTC price (as of February 2018).

BITCOIN HISTORY

BItcoin has been around since 2009, and in that time it has seen a fair amount of mystery, intrigue, growth, and challenges. For such a relatively young technology, Bitcoin has a complex and compelling history.

THE STORY OF SATOSHI

Bitcoin started with a white paper written by a mysterious author, Satoshi Nakamoto. In the white paper, Satoshi outlined the basic elements of blockchain technology. He/she/they showed how to use hashing to create blocks and drive proof of work, solving the double spend problem. The white paper was well received in the relatively small crypto community of the time, but there was one problem. Nobody had ever heard of Satoshi Nakamoto, and nobody could find anything about this mysterious person.

Satoshi continued to interact via forums and emails, but no one could ever figure out who the real person behind the pseudonym was. In 2009, Satoshi wrote the code behind Bitcoin and launched the network to the world. For years, Satoshi continued as the lead developer on Bitcoin until 2011 when he abruptly disappeared. Over the years, several people have claimed to be Satoshi, but nothing definitive has been found on the inventor of Bitcoin.

It is clear that Satoshi was brilliant. Inventing blockchain solved a huge cryptographic hurdle in creating a viable distributed ledger. Even if Bitcoin were to fail tomorrow, blockchain technology is already in use for hundreds of applications, not just as a currency. It may go down in history that Satoshi was among the most important inventors of the 21st century, and we don't know anything about him/her/them.

Satoshi transferred control of Bitcoin's development to Gavin Andresen upon his disappearance. Andresen went on to become the lead developer at the Bitcoin Foundation, the organization currently responsible for Bitcoin development.

SILK ROAD SEIZURE

As Bitcoin began to gather steam, its anonymous wallets made it the perfect tool for conducting legally questionable transactions. Bitcoin's first few years were marked by this reputation as a black market, drug money, or money laundering currency.

In October 2013, the FBI raided the home of Ross William Ulbricht under charges of being the founder of a darknet website known as the Silk Road. The Silk Road had become notorious as a place to purchase illegal drugs online. As part of the seizure, the FBI also seized roughly 26,000 Bitcoins, marking one of the first official interactions between the U.S. government and the Bitcoin network.

Overall, the Silk Road incident was bad press for the Bitcoin network, further driving home the idea of Bitcoin as a currency for illegal activities.

THE MT. GOX MYSTERY

One of the earliest Bitcoin exchanges was Mt. Gox, a Tokyo-based company that was one of the major exchanges in the early days of Bitcoin. Mt. Gox's CEO, Mark Karpeles, was CEO in name only and much preferred coding to the day-to-day challenges of being CEO.

In 2014, Mt. Gox was the world's largest Bitcoin exchange, handling over 70% of Bitcoin transactions worldwide. So, it came as a shock to consumers when Mt. Gox filed for bankruptcy in 2014. Over the course of years, its system had been hacked. In all, $450 million worth of Bitcoin disappeared from Mt. Gox's accounts between 2011 and 2014. While investigators were able to find some 200,000 BTC involved in the Mt. Gox hack, over 650,000 BTC were not recovered.

During the period of the Mt. Gox hack, Bitcoin decreased 36% in value.

It should be noted that the problem was not with Bitcoin technology, but Mt. Gox's security procedures. While Bitcoin's open ledger means those coins have been "found," there's no clear way to take the coins from their current owners and return them to their original owners.

To this day, Mt. Gox remains the biggest scandal in Bitcoin history, and it sparked a period of serious doubt over the cryptocurrency's viability.

CENTRALIZATION OF MINING

A more recent concern in the history of Bitcoin is the centralization of mining. Bitcoin's proof of work algorithm is written in such a way that hardware manufacturers have developed Bitcoin-specific processing chips to earn the lucrative mining rewards. As Bitcoin's price has skyrocketed in recent years, the arms race for more and faster chips has accelerated.

At this point, Bitcoin mining is a professional operation, with mining companies investing hundreds of thousands of dollars in mining hardware "farms." These farms of hundreds of mining computers are often enormous, even filling entire warehouses with mining computers.

This growth in mining makes it unprofitable for small-time miners to compete, centralizing power among a few mega-miners. Unfortunately this means the network that was created to be decentralized is paradoxically centralized. Miners could decide to prioritize certain types of transactions or blacklist certain users from the Bitcoin network.

There's no clear evidence that Bitcoin miners are abusing their power yet, however. This is largely because a few changes in Bitcoin's underlying code could make the expensive mining hardware worthless. As such, there's a strong incentive to be honest and keep the Bitcoin community and Bitcoin Foundation happy.

Bitcoin's Scalability Problem

In 2017, Bitcoin is more popular than ever. Bitcoin's rapid growth in valuation over the past year has fueled wide public awareness of the currency. It has also encouraged a lot of speculation, with investors buying and selling Bitcoin in the hopes of turning a profit or avoiding a crash.

This increased interest in Bitcoin means the network saw a 55% increase in transaction volume (http://bit.ly/2su1xGg) in 2017. On the average day, the Bitcoin network processes 310,000 transactions (https://blockchain.info/charts). However, the network isn't meeting demand. On any given day, there are tens of thousands of transactions that get put on hold waiting for the network to catch up to confirm them.

These transactions are on hold because Bitcoin has a limit on its block size. Only so many transactions can fit in one block, so any that don't fit have to wait. This waiting for confirmation is Bitcoin's scalability problem, and it's one that must be solved before the coin will be feasible as an everyday currency.

Wait Times and Fees for Processing

Current wait times range from a few minutes to several hours for your transaction to be approved on the blockchain. This is problematic because we've become accustomed to instant payments and verification. If I have to wait several hours between ordering something and payment, then it makes time-sensitive transactions impossible on Bitcoin.

In response, mining companies have offered to prioritize transactions that pay them a fee. If you want your transaction processed quicker, you'll need to pay for it. Bitcoin was originally designed to be frictionless and free. It was also meant to avoid central authority. When miners charge fees for transactions, it feels very similar to banks charging processing fees, one of the very things Bitcoin was developed to avoid.

RESTRICTED BLOCK SIZE AND SEGWIT2X

Bitcoin's block size is currently limited to 1 MB. All the transaction and confirmation info has to be less than (or close to) 1 MB for the block to be accepted.

The debate around how to increase Bitcoin's scalability boils down to increasing the information you can fit in a block. One solution is to decrease the amount of information you put inside the block. In the case of Bitcoin, this takes the form of separating the transaction data from the electronic signatures that authorize the transaction. Removing the signatures from the block and processing them separately means you can fit more transactions in the block. This decoupling of signatures from their transactions is called segregated witness (SegWit), and this technology is currently deployed on the Bitcoin blockchain. Some miners are using it, while others are using the old way. If SegWit really proves to be better, the idea is eventually 100% of the network will use it.

There is another way to increase the amount of information you can fit in a block. Simply increase the size of the block. There is a movement to double the size of the Bitcoin block to 2 MB. This is the newest effort in Bitcoin, known as 2x, and when combined with SegWit, it could mean an enormous increase in Bitcoin's ability to process transactions. SegWit2x is a huge change to the architecture underlying Bitcoin, and the implications aren't entirely clear for how it will affect the ecosystem as a whole.

In November 2017, the implementation of SegWit2x stalled. There simply isn't a strong enough consensus in the Bitcoin community behind such a change to the Bitcoin base code. While it's on hold for now, SegWit2x is not dead by any means, and we could see it return in the future as Bitcoin continues to work on scalability.

CONCLUSIONS ABOUT BITCOIN

Bitcoin is the mother of all blockchain, and it continues to be the preeminent cryptocurrency in the world. It is the most established and strongest of the cryptocurrencies out there. However, there are other contenders in the blockchain industry, and it's not a sure thing that Bitcoin will end up the winner when all is said and done. Bitcoin needs to address its scalability issues and increase adoption if it wants to maintain its dominance.

WHAT IS ETHEREUM AND WHY IS IT IMPORTANT?

Ethereum is the second-biggest cryptocurrency in the world after Bitcoin. It's also very different from Bitcoin in its structure and purpose. Ethereum wasn't developed as a currency alone. Its innovation lies in opening the blockchain up to development for different applications outside currencies and finance.

Developers can build software on top of Ethereum's blockchain, and use the network's distributed ledger to build trust for all kinds of applications. Since the Ethereum blockchain is decentralized, once a developer has built an application, it can't be censored or taken down by any authority. That application lives as long as the Ethereum blockchain continues.

This has huge implications for agreements, contracts, and conditional transactions. They can be programmed, automated, and set in stone so neither party can cheat. Using the blockchain for such transactions and contracts builds trust because the peer network verifies all the information and doesn't allow for alterations after the fact.

ETHEREUM'S BRIEF HISTORY

Ethereum's white paper, released in 2013, described a system whereby the blockchain could be opened up to a scripting language for application development. Vitalik Buterin, one of the founders and lead programmer of Ethereum, had a longstanding history writing about Bitcoin. He advocated for a scripting language on top of the Bitcoin blockchain, but it would require rewriting the Bitcoin base code to be compatible for programming languages. When this proved controversial, he decided to create a new blockchain that would allow the creation of autonomous applications.

Buterin's Ethereum project began development in 2014, funded by a crowdsale. Essentially, the Ethereum developers launched a crowdfunding campaign where backers would receive a stake in the company, in the form of tokens that would power the apps built on Ethereum. These tokens were called Ether (ETH), and the crowdsale allowed backers to buy Ether in exchange for Bitcoin.

At the time, the crypto-tech community was interested in the idea of decentralized applications, and the Ethereum launch generated significant buzz. However, many were understandably concerned about the security risks of creating a platform where users could code their own applications. Other skeptics raised concerns about Ethereum's scalability, as many autonomous apps running on the blockchain would require more computing power.

The Switzerland-based Ethereum Foundation released the first prototype version of Ethereum in May 2015 and challenged test users to find bugs and limitations in the system. In July of the same year, the Foundation released the first official version of Ethereum for public use known as Frontier.

Ethereum has since released two new versions of the platform, with Ethereum's current version (November 2017) known as Metropolis.

THE DAO HACK

One of the core features of the Ethereum blockchain is applications can be built on top of the Ethereum blockchain. One of the most popular projects to be built on the Ethereum blockchain was the Decentralized Autonomous Organization (DAO). The DAO was a crypto currency and venture funding project. It was meant to revolutionize consensus decision making and voting, allowing people from around the world to fund various projects through DAO in a form of decentralized venture capital.

The DAO quickly raised ~$150 million (http://nyti.ms/2Hk8TQ2) upon its creation in 2016. However, applications built on the Ethereum blockchain are only as secure as their underlying code. In May, computer scientists pointed out vulnerabilities in the underlying code, and soon thereafter the DAO reported hackers had siphoned more than $50 million from the DAO. The DAO had been one of the most successful crowdsales ever, and it was seen as the standard bearer for decentralization and the promise of cryptocurrencies. The DAO hack, and subsequent shutdown of the DAO, rattled those notions.

In response to the enormous DAO hack, the Ethereum Foundation proposed a hard fork to move the stolen funds back to their original owners. This new fork went into effect shortly after the DAO hack and became the new official version of Ethereum. However, some users opposed to the ethics and precedent of centrally controlling money and using central authority to change transactions, continued to maintain that the old blockchain was the true Ethereum. This blockchain with no alterations after DAO is known as Ethereum Classic.

SMART CONTRACTS

The basic building block of Ethereum's decentralized platform is the smart contract. These are agreements that execute on their own based on different variables. Deploying smart contracts on the blockchain has a few advantages.

First, since blockchains are decentralized, there's

no need to pay or trust a middleman with your transaction. Second, blockchain smart contracts are more secure, since changing the terms of the contract would require writing new blocks faster than the network can (statistically nearly impossible). FInally, blockchain smart contracts can execute faster than a middleman.

The essence of the smart contract is if all parties in the contract uphold their ends of the bargain, then the contract will automatically execute. If one of the parties fails to uphold the contract, then it automatically returns the funds, value, information, goods, etc to their original owners. In essence, smart contracts work like an escrow service, taking in funds and holding them until the other party in the contract upholds their end of the deal.

DECENTRALIZED AUTONOMOUS ORGANIZATIONS

While the DAO (discussed above) is one example of a decentralized autonomous organization, there are many others. Essentially, autonomous organizations use a series of smart contracts to execute goals that would have otherwise been handled by an institution.

For instance, DAOs could be used in voting, education, insurance, healthcare, and music sales. They could deliver files, manage records, collect funds, monitor patients, and track the progress of projects. Smart contracts would allow these organizations to act as soon as and only if certain conditions are met.

The advantage of DAOs is they don't play favorites and they operate on transparent rules and guidelines. They're also cheap to operate, and transactions are frictionless. Smart contracts and DAOs are exciting advancements in blockchain technology, because they could replace all kinds of institutions, not just financial institutions.

ETHEREUM ICOS AND THE ERC-20 TOKEN PROTOCOL

The explosion of dApps, DAOs, and other programs on the Ethereum network meant that many types of value exchange were happening on Ethereum at once. While some of these applications used Ether as their means of exchange, others wanted more control over the token used to drive transactions in their apps/DAOs. It became common for every new application on Ethereum to also develop a new token to power the application.

The reason for the growth in new tokens boils down to the concept of an initial coin offering (ICO). When someone has a new idea, they need funding to create and implement the application. Over the past year, it has become common for new ideas to get funded by selling new tokens in exchange for Ethereum. These crowdsales allow anyone to invest in an idea and buy a share of that idea's worth. If the idea works out, the value of the newly created token will increase and early investors will be rewarded.

2017 has been the year of ICOs. According to Bloomberg (https://bloom.bg/2F4Vk68), ICOs have raised over $1.6 billion in 2017 alone. The explosion of ICOs is a result of the ease with which Ethereum permits the creation of new coins. With little more than an idea and a white paper, you can set up an Ethereum-based ICO and raise millions of dollars, circumventing the old-school fundraising channels of venture capital or seed funding from institutional investors.

An ICO works much the same way as a Kickstarter campaign. Backer contribute digital currency (usually Ether) to the ICO's smart contract. If the project reaches its funding goal, the smart contract distributes the new tokens to the backers and deposits the Ether into the developer's account to begin creating the new idea. If the project fails it's funding goals, all the backers receive a refund.

Ethereum has become the go-to place to create new ICOs for a few reasons. First, the blockchain already exists and you don't have to code a new blockchain from scratch. Second, Ethereum has a huge mining community and the second largest market cap of any cryptocurrency, making for a strong foundation for a new project. Finally, Ethereum has a clear set of guidelines for creating new tokens called the ERC-20 protocol.

The ERC-20 protocol also means that all the tokens on Ethereum are now exchangeable. Before ERC-20, each developer wrote their own arguments and functions. Exchanging one token for another often required studying the code and building a bridge between the two tokens for the exchange. Since ERC-20, however, all arguments and functions are standardized, and new tokens on Ethereum can immediately be exchanged for any other ERC-20 compatible token.

ETHEREUM'S MOVE TO PROOF OF STAKE

Over the past year or so, the Ethereum Foundation has increasingly indicated that it intends to move Ethereum away from proof of work verification toward proof of stake. Remember, proof of work is a system where thousands of mining computers compete to solve a cryptographic puzzle. In proof of stake, however, all those miners go away. Instead, the users who own Ethereum verify the transactions on the network. If they verify them correctly, they receive a reward. If they verify them incorrectly, they lose all their Ether (their stake).

With proof of stake, only one CPU is chosen to be the "verifier" at a time. That CPU is chosen based on how much Ether it is associated with. Someone who owns 1% of the Ether in the world would have a 1% chance of being chosen as the verifier. (1% of the Ethereum network is nothing to sneeze at. That would be worth about $300 million out of Ethereum's $30 billion market cap.)

The verifier in a proof of stake system is weighted by their stake in the network, but the selection is also randomized. This ensures that a coordinated attack couldn't create multiple falsified blocks in a row. Since the verifier risks losing all their Ether, there's a strong incentive to act honestly.

WHY MAKE THE MOVE?

Proof of work is an excellent system with proven results in ensuring blockchain security, so why switch? There are two factors driving Ethereum's switch to proof of stake: energy consumption and demand for fiat currency.

Ethereum uses an anti-ASIC hashing algorithm, meaning it hasn't seen the warehouses of specialized mining equipment running day and night that Bitcoin has. However, Ethereum's small-time mining operations still consume significant amounts of electricity. Ultimately, blockchain technologies hope to be ubiquitous, powering every part of society. It's simply not feasible long term for blockchain to continue to use proof of work, as electricity demands will outstrip the world's ability to produce extra power. Proof of stake enthusiasts also point out that mining usually happens in countries with low electricity costs where less of the grid is powered by renewables, contributing to fossil fuel consumption and global warming.

The other factor behind proof of stake is more self-interested. Since electricity bills are paid in fiat currency, cryptocurrency mining is paradoxically supporting the use of fiat. Proof of stake vastly reduces the required electricity, meaning verifiers won't have to cash out their Ethereum in order to pay their electricity bills.

WHEN WILL IT HAPPEN?

The question of when Ethereum will implement proof of stake doesn't yet have an answer. For most of this year Vitalik Buterin and the Ethereum Foundation team have been answering, "Soon".

The test of proof of stake comes in the form of Casper (http://bit.ly/2Eun6ff), Buterin's proposed overhaul to the Ethereum base code. In the beginning, proof of stake would only verify 1 in 100 blocks in order to test the technology's viability. Over time, the use of proof of stake would ramp up until it reaches 100%.

As of September 2017, Buterin was formalizing

his plans (https://www.coindesk.com/ethereum-seeing-ghosts-vitalik-buterin-is-finally-formalizingethereums-casper-upgrade/) for Casper into a series of white papers for the community to review. Casper would go into effect shortly thereafter in 2018. However, given previous delays on the move to proof of stake, that timeline could be changed.

ARE THERE OTHER BLOCKCHAIN TECHNOLOGIES TO KEEP AN EYE ON?

Bitcoin and Ethereum are the largest and most notable blockchain technologies, but there are hundreds of other projects currently operating or under development. This summarizes some of these up-and-coming projects and their potential uses.

BITCOIN CASH

Bitcoin Cash is an offshoot of the Bitcoin blockchain using the same source code, but it is a separate currency from Bitcoin. It is now the third most valuable cryptocurrency in the world in terms of market cap, behind Bitcoin and Ethereum. Bitcoin Cash diverged from Bitcoin when members of the Bitcoin community disagreed about how to address Bitcoin's scalability problem. The result was a procedure known as a "hard fork," where Bitcoin Cash created a new blockchain that shares the same transaction history as Bitcoin up to a certain point. At that point, the hard fork created two separate blockchains that run parallel to each other. Users who held Bitcoin before the hard fork held an identical amount of Bitcoin Cash after the fork, but the coins are not interchangeable and are not connected.

What changed in the new Bitcoin Cash blockchain was the block size limit. Bitcoin only allows blocks to reach 1 MB in size. This means any transactions that don't fit in the 1 MB size limit get put on hold. With Bitcoin's rise in popularity, a lot of transactions are getting put on hold, and users have resorted to paying fees to miners in order to have their transactions included in the block. The Bitcoin Cash hard fork increased the block size to 8 MB, allowing the blockchain to accommodate many more transactions and seeking to solve the scalability problem. Bitcoin Cash's founders and users are banking on the Bitcoin community's inability to come to a consensus regarding scalability, making Bitcoin Cash an increasingly more attractive option and eventually dethroning Bitcoin altogether.

LITECOIN

Litecoin is an older cryptocurrency that was launched 2011, shortly after Bitcoin's launch in 2009. The differences between Litecoin and Bitcoin are relatively small. Both rely on a decentralized ledger with proof of work mining. The difference is the time it takes to create a new block on each network. For Bitcoin, it takes about 10 minutes for miners to create a new block. For Litecoin, it only takes about 2 minutes.

The simple change in block times does have some significant effects. For instance, because it creates new blocks more frequently, Litecoin can process more transactions than Bitcoin. Additionally, new transactions get added to the ledger and confirmed much more quickly on Litecoin. Confirmation that's 6 blocks deep (extremely low probability of ever being altered or double spent by an attacker) would take only 12 minutes on Litecoin, whereas the same confirmation would take around an hour on Bitcoin. The faster confirmations makes Litecoin more merchant-friendly.

Litecoin's frequent creation of blocks has the drawback of making Litecoin's blockchain much larger than Bitcoin's, requiring more storage from anyone who wants to run a node. However, due to the block frequency and high overall money supply of Litecoin, transactions on the Litecoin blockchain charge much lower fees than on Bitcoin. Faster confirmations and lower fees present a great use case for Litecoin. However, it has failed to overtake Bitcoin in the past 6 years based on technological improvements alone, and there are many more new currencies entering the arena.

PRIVACY COINS: ZCASH & MONERO

Privacy is a growing concern in the cryptocurrency community. Since blockchain relies on a public ledger, anyone can observe how transactions are moving and the amounts being paid. While Bitcoin wallets are technically anonymous, if you can learn someone's public address or trace a web of transactions to a person, you can track that person's spending. This raises all kinds of concerns about traceability, even if you're not engaged in questionable behaviors.

Privacy and untraceability fosters fungibility in a currency. Fungibility means that a currency has value on its own, without regard to the transaction history. Cash is fungible because when you hand a shop owner a dollar, the owner doesn't ask you where you got the dollar. On Bitcoin, certain coins have been blacklisted because they've been involved in illicit activities in the past. With true privacy coins you don't have blacklists or rejected coins because the transaction history for the coin is hidden.

MONERO

The mechanisms by which Monero and Zcash ensure untraceability are different. Monero uses two technologies - ring confidential transactions and stealth addresses - to hide the sender, recipient, and amount of the transaction. Essentially, if Alice wants to send Monero (XMR) to Bob, she randomly selects a few other wallets where the money she's sending Bob might have come from. Using some complex cryptography, these wallets begin transacting to form a "ring" such that when the money finally leaves for Bob, it's not clear which wallet in the ring authorized the transaction.

With Monero, the funds don't go directly to Bob, though. Instead, they get deposited in a "stealth address," which is essentially an empty locker with no identifying information. Bob has a special key that allows him to see which lockers (stealth addresses) are meant for him, and when he wants to spend the contents of one of those lockers, the process starts over again with a new ring confidential transaction.

In this way, Alice and Bob's information never reaches the blockchain. It's all stealth addresses that are transacting in rings at all times, making it impossible to trace the flow of funds through the noise and difficult to identify who owns which stealth address.

ZCASH

Zcash's untraceability technology works a little differently. It uses a system of cryptographic tests known as a zero knowledge proof. The purpose of a zero knowledge proof is to verify a transaction without knowing anything about what's going on inside the transaction. The way it works involves three components: a generated key (G) that serves as a test, a proving key (P) that shows the prover can answer the test, and a verifying key (V) to verify the prover's answer.

When Adam wants to send Zcash to Betty, he receives a publicly generated key (G) from the system.

Adam then uses the information about the transaction (his address, Betty's address, and the transaction amount) plus his special prover key, and combines that information with G. The system then analyzes his response using V. If the transaction Adam proposed is valid, then V will be true. If the transaction is invalid, V will be false. The system will propose a few of these tests with different generated keys (G). While Adam might have been able to guess correctly once, due to the cryptography behind the zero knowledge proof, he won't be able to consistently answer correctly unless his transaction is valid.

Because verifiers don't need to know the details of a transaction in order to know it's true, the Zcash blockchain ledger doesn't have to include identifiable information. However, hiding the sender, recipient, or both on Zcash is optional and not turned on by default.

Monero and Zcash are at the forefront of the privacy movement to fix these traceability issues in Bitcoin. Monero uses cryptographic technologies known as stealth addresses and ring confidential transactions to keep the sender, recipient, and amount of transactions hidden from the public blockchain. Zcash on the other hand utilizes zero knowledge proofs to allow miners to verify transactions without having to know anything about what's inside those transactions.

The rising interest in privacy has also led Ethereum to adopt zero-knowledge proofs for its transactions.

DASH

Dash is based off the Bitcoin software, but it's designed to solve some of the inherent flaws in the Bitcoin network. The guiding principle behind Dash is user-friendliness, and helping new users easily join the world of cryptocurrencies. Dash makes a few key changes to the way Bitcoin operated.

For starters, Dash is another privacy coin with measures in place to prevent Bitcoin's traceability problem. Dash accomplishes its untraceability using one of the earliest forms of obfuscation, coin mixing. The idea is simple. If everyone put their coins into a pot, mixed the pot, and then redrew the same amount of funds as they put in, then they'd have the same amount of money but it would be incredibly difficult to tell who got what money from where.

The challenge is the mixing requires some type of honest coordinator who will mix the pot fairly and redistribute everyone's coins properly. In Dash, the coordinator for the network is a group of power users known as masternodes. While Dash still relies on miners to do the proof of work for the blockchain, the Dash algorithm shares part of the block reward for each new block with the masternodes as well. These masternodes assist with the coin mixing that happens every 10 blocks. They also facilitate transactions that can be confirmed instantly. With Dash, you no longer have to wait for several blocks to go by before your transaction is confirmed. Instead, the masternodes help secure and monitor the transactions you want to send instantly. Dash calls this feature InstantX, and you can turn it on or off on your Dash transactions, for a fee.

Dash also supports services that allow you to link a debit card to your Bitcoin or Dash wallet. These debit cards are pre-paid, but they convert from BTC to your local currency automatically and on-demand when you want to refill the card. Essentially allowing you to hold your bank savings in Bitcoin and convert to local currency only when you need it. While this type of service is way ahead of its time, it's possible blockchain-based currencies could become the default place to keep money in the near future.

The changes Dash made to Bitcoin's user-friendliness: privacy, instant payments, and a two-tiered network, make Dash a compelling competitor to Bitcoin. As of writing, Dash is the fifth most valuable cryptocurrency in the world, and its adoption is growing.

HYPERLEDGER

Hyperledger is not a currency, not a company, and not even a blockchain. It's a project from the same people behind Linux operating system. The idea is to develop blockchain and cryptographic applications that are open source. Hyperledger hopes to be the hub of blockchain development, a clearinghouse for the best open-source technologies.

The folks at Hyperledger are simply excited about the possible applications of blockchain. Not since the invention of the internet have we seen a technology that has the potential to radically alter how we think about institutions, information, and value transfer. Based on that belief, the Linux Foundation started the Hyperledger project in 2015. It's the place where major companies in tech and finance come to be a part of the development of blockchain. So far, the Hyperledger project has the support of Samsung, Intel, IBM, Airbus, CISCO, American Express, JP Morgan, and more.

The thinking is in order for blockchain to be useful long term, we need to explore many possible applications for the technology and make access to blockchain information as equitable as possible. Hyperledger believes it's possible that blockchain could impact everything we do in our daily lives, and guaranteeing a neutral, open platform for the new technology makes sure everyone benefits and no one gets left out.

Instead of creating a coin, like many other blockchain projects, Hyperledger is focused on creating projects and platforms. They're laying the groundwork and infrastructure for future blockchain-based project by creating code bases, libraries, conventions, standards, frameworks, and tools that make blockchain development easier and faster.

IOTA

IOTA stands for Internet of Things Application, and it hopes to be the infrastructure for billions of smart devices - like sensors, cameras, and gauges - that are and will be connected to the internet. These smart devices need access to resources like electricity, bandwidth, data storage, and computing power, but there's currently no way for them to share these resources across the internet of things.

IOTA's vision is enabling devices to communicate and buy resources from one another using microtransactions at fractions of a penny. In order to facilitate a fast, frictionless, and free microtransaction system, IOTA has done away with the blockchain. Instead, they use a related cryptographic technology known as directed acyclic graph (DAG) to create a complex web of transactions. In order to post a new transaction on IOTA, you must verify two other transactions first. IOTA calls its DAG chain "The Tangle." Much of the IOTA infrastructure is new and relatively untested, so there's cause for concern. However, if the developers can pull off a working system, they could create a whole new economy of free microtransactions that was previously impossible because of transaction fees.

RIPPLE

Ripple is a platform for cross-border payments and a currency to facilitate those payments. What makes Ripple different from other cryptocurrencies is they aren't seeking to overthrow the current system of financial institutions. Instead, Ripple is selling itself as a payment solution and liquidity provider for banks and payment processors.

Payments, especially across borders, are slow and expensive. Banks haven't caught up with the technological revolution in has given us the internet and immediate access to information. In fact, bank transfers still take days to process and often require expensive fees. Ripple uses the cryptography from blockchain, deployed on a network of trusted verifiers, to enable instant payments for banks with lower fees and liquidity requirements.

The idea behind Ripple is to act as infrastructure for existing financial institutions. Where many other cryptocurrencies are trying to displace or compete with financial institutions, Ripple is embracing these institutions and offers a blockchain-based way to process transactions that's more efficient. It seems to be working. Ripple has already gained adoption from over 100 financial institutions, including American Express, and with continued adoption Ripple could become an industry standard for payments.

Ripple's currency is the fourth most valuable cryptocurrency in the world as of writing. This is largely due to the high demand for Ripple as a way to settle payments between banks that operate with different currencies. Using the RippleNet, the banks can transfer and settle accounts in fiat currencies, like dollars or pounds, but they can just as easily use Ripple's currency to settle the debts within the system.

CORPORATE ADOPTION

Hyperledger, IOTA, and Ripple - along with Ethereum's smart contracts - show the potential of blockchain technologies outside the strict realm of cryptocurrency. Blockchain is a technology that works faster and uses less resources than current systems in many industries.

As a result, companies are implementing their own

internal, private blockchain solutions that use their current computing power and network of offices and data centers more efficiently. Microsoft is developing Project Bletchley, an open, modular Blockchain-as-a-service that businesses can use alongside technologies like Azure to power their enterprise software and server needs. Accenture and JP Morgan are working on enterprise distributed ledgers with added features for permission and security. IBM also offers enterprise blockchain services.

Of course banks are considering ways that blockchain could power payments, and a collective of banks has met to try to do something similar to what Ripple is already doing for payment infrastructure. Outside of finance, leaders in artificial intelligence are considering ways to use the computing power of blockchain mining for training machine learning algorithms on large datasets. Blockchain holds huge promise in cybersecurity, since it makes systems that are append-only, and cryptographically very difficult to edit later. We'll likely see blockchain applied in supply chain management, since inventories and order requests are still ledgers that can easily be added to blocks. Similarly, health care and patient records could be revolutionized with blockchain that can store data anonymously and only reveal it when a patient presents his doctor with a private view key.

The applications are exciting and seemingly endless for blockchain and it's difficult to know how completely blockchain technology will revolutionize our world and how long it might take.

WILL BLOCKCHAIN dAPPS AND DAOS CHANGE EVERYTHING?

Blockchain enthusiasts paint a picture of the world where institutions have lost and blockchain has won. Everything from your bank account to your car insurance to voting is now done on the blockchain via decentralized autonomous organizations and applications. Because of this decentralization, institutions no longer have sway over our decisions or data about us. Our lives are more efficient because transactions are quicker and cheaper and safer because the network creates trust between strangers.

On the other hand, blockchain detractors believe the technology is a bubble, over-hyped and not as revolutionary as its fans predict. Anyone who believes that today's powerful institutions are going to allow themselves to be overthrown is naive. While the technology will get used, it will help major institutions earn wider profit margins without changing the life experience of the average person much at all.

In truth, the real future of blockchain is somewhere in the middle. Most people don't appreciate that blockchain technology is still in its infancy, and it won't be ready to solve huge global problems for another 5-10 years. When it does reach that maturity, it will likely get implemented by large corporations and institutions. It will help them earn more money, and it will make our lives more efficient as well.

The crux of the matter is blockchain still isn't useful yet. Even with the rising prices of cryptocurrencies, they're not anywhere near mainstream, and it's difficult to use them to buy anything useful, much less pay your rent or electricity bill. While the technology has huge potential, it still will require intensive development before it becomes mainstream. It will probably also fail, sometimes in spectacular ways, before it succeeds.

DECENTRALIZATION HAS THE POTENTIAL TO REVOLUTIONIZE LIFE AS WE KNOW IT

The digital era began with personal computers decentralizing processing power. The earliest PCs meant anyone could use computers to answer questions and create new content. The internet decentralized information. Now, anyone in the world can find information on almost any topic using a quick Google search, leading to an explosion in knowledge and creativity. The blockchain will decentralize trust, and that's no small achievement.

When two strangers can do business or exchange value anywhere in the world for free, it fundamentally changes the way the global economy operates. The lack of barriers makes it easy for me to create a contract with someone in Nigeria, Tibet, or Fiji from my home, and because of the way smart contracts are constructed, I know that I won't be scammed out or my money. The contract will not pay until the terms of the contract are met. Trust is a core human problem, from governance to news, payments, healthcare, and transportation. We need to be able to trust strangers, like your airplane pilot or your local police officer, and the blockchain helps with that.

REGULATORY HURDLES

Of course the implementation of blockchain technologies isn't without its hurdles, and government regulation seems to be foremost among them. Governments have real concerns about identity, trust, and validation when it comes to their citizens. A technology that creates trust without needing identity or citizenship is a threat to government itself, but it also makes it difficult to enforce certain laws, especially when it comes to dangerous materials, drugs, and other types of illicit trafficking.

With the current cryptocurrency growth, governments are understandably worried about anti-money laundering laws that were put in place to stop criminals and terrorists from washing illegal funds. These groups could invest in a privacy cryptocurrency, move the money around in an untraceable way, and then withdraw it from a different account. For this reason, most governments have put in place know your customer regulations that apply to the exchanges that convert cryptocurrencies to fiat currencies (dollars/pounds/yen).

Similarly, governments are worried about the ways smart contracts might be used to create business deals that would otherwise be considered illegal. When these contracts are negotiated through lawyers and banks, the government has a means to intervene with the coordinating institution. However, with institution-less contracts, it becomes more difficult for the government to monitor and verify the legality of every smart contract.

As blockchain grows in popularity, so will the number of regulations regarding how it can be used. But the central challenge is trying to regulate something that's decentralized. I think we'd all agree that we don't want blockchain used to do harm, but how do you enforce that? And who decides what's harmful? These questions are ethical, but they also don't have a clear way for the government to intervene. As the government tries to create ways to intervene, it could jeopardize the decentralization of blockchain that made it such a useful technology in the first place, making blockchain regulation a no-win scenario.

THE POSSIBLE FUTURE INTERNET, POWERED BY BLOCKCHAIN

We've reached the end, and I hope you've enjoyed this deep dive into all things blockchain. Of course, there are hundreds of blockchain-based projects this short book couldn't address, and the technical details of each project are fascinating themselves. If you found this book interesting, I recommend you dive deeper into different books and websites so you can put what you've learned here into context. I specifically recommend learning more about cryptography and how it enables the whole blockchain ecosystem.

Over the coming years, the early technologies described in this book will eventually begin to look childish compared to the future applications of blockchain. Much like static websites in the 1990s bear no resemblance to today's highly interactive web-based applications, so too will blockchain projects grow in complexity and user-friendliness. Eventually, we'll all be using blockchain-based technologies as part of everyday life. It will integrate seamlessly with the rest of our lives, and it will make life a little bit easier for everyone.

ABOUT THE AUTHOR

Alan T. Norman is a proud, savvy, and ethical hacker from San Francisco City. After receiving a Bachelor's of Science at Stanford University. Alan now works for a mid-sizc Informational Tcchnology Firm in the heart of SFC. He aspires to work for the United States government as a security hacker, but also loves teaching others about the future of technology. Alan firmly believes that the future will heavily rely computer "geeks" for both security and the successes of companies and future jobs alike. In his spare time, he loves to analyze and scrutinize everything about the game of basketball.

CRYPTOCURRENCY MINING BONUS BOOK

FIND THE LINK TO THE BONUS BOOK BELOW

www.erdpublishing.com/cryptocurrency-mining-bonus/

OTHER BOOKS BY ALAN T. NORMAN:
Mastering Bitcoin for Starters
(http://amzn.to/2AwSNy0)

Cryptocurrency Investing Bible

(http://amzn.to/2zzB8IP)

Hacking: Computer Hacking Beginners Guide

(www.amazon.com/dp/B01N4FFHMW)

Hacking: How to Make Your Own Keylogger in C++ Programming Language

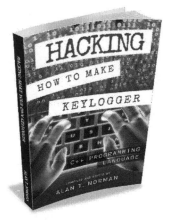

HACKED: Kali Linux and Wireless Hacking Ultimate Guide
(https://www.amazon.com/dp/B0791WS RNZ)

Contributors

Thank you to Bennett Garner who provided insightful feedback, careful edits, moral support, and gentle prodding.

I am in awe of his willingness to contribute to making this book what it is.

ONE LAST THING...

DID YOU ENJOY THE BOOK?

IF SO, THEN LET ME KNOW BY LEAVING A REVIEW ON AMAZON! Reviews are the lifeblood of independent authors. I would appreciate even a few words and rating if that's all you have time for

IF YOU DID NOT LIKE THIS BOOK, THEN PLEASE TELL ME! Email me at alannormanit@gmail.com and let me know what you didn't like! Perhaps I can change it. In today's world a book doesn't have to be stagnant, it can improve with time and feedback from readers like you. You can impact this book, and I welcome your feedback. Help make this book better for everyone!